Strong and Sturdy
Dramas for Children

Lisa Gaylord, Barbara Hollenbach,
Chad Hoover, Cheryl Kirking

All Scripture quotations, unless otherwise indicated, are taken from the HOLY BIBLE, NEW INTERNATIONAL VERSION®. NIV®. Copyright © 1973, 1978, 1984 by International Bible Society. Used by permission of Zondervan Publishing House. All rights reserved.

Copyright © 1999 Concordia Publishing House
3558 S. Jefferson Avenue, St. Louis, MO 63118-3968
Manufactured in the United States of America

Educational institutions, teachers, or churches who purchase this product may reproduce pages for classroom use, for use in parish-education programs, or for use in worship settings. Material is intended for use by purchaser in the purchaser's local church only. As the purchaser, you may make as many copies of the scripts as are needed for performance in your local church only. You may perform the sketches as often as you wish at no additional cost. Scripts and performance rights are not transferable between churches and cannot be resold. You may not use the sketches for any commercial or fundraising purpose, and usage rights do not extend to video, radio, television, or film.

All rights reserved. Except as noted above, no part of this publication may be reproduced, stored in a retrieval system, or transmitted, in any form or by any means, electronic, mechanical, photocopying, recording, or otherwise, without the prior written permission of Concordia Publishing House.

1 2 3 4 5 6 7 8 9 10   08 07 06 05 04 03 02 01 00 99

Contents

Introduction	5
Production Notes: Using Drama with Children	7
Production Notes: Using Sketches	13
1. Shadrach, Meshach, and Abednego *Chad Hoover* 5–7 minute sketch	15
2. Strong and Sturdy *Lisa Gaylord* 7–10 minute sketch	27
3. Giving God Glory *Cheryl Kirking* 3–5 minute sketch	37
Production Notes: Using Full-length Plays and Programs	43
4. What's a Nice Jewish Girl Like You Doing in a Persian Harem? *Barbara Hollenbach* One act play based on the story of Esther	44

Introduction

Fix these words of mine in your hearts and minds .... Teach them to your children, talking about them when you sit at home and when you walk along the road, when you lie down and when you get up. Deuteronomy 11:18–19

What images do the words "strong and sturdy" conjure? Something unbreakable perhaps, or enduring: rocks, fortresses, large trees. But children?

The idea is even more absurd considering the note Webster adds to the definition: "Strong may imply power derived from muscular vigor, large size, structural soundness, intellectual or spiritual resources. Sturdy implies strength derived from vigorous growth, determination of spirit, solidity of construction."

Children often aren't considered strong in terms of their muscular vigor, size, or structural soundness. Most are overlooked in terms of their intellectual resources, and most, unfortunately, are overlooked in terms of their spiritual resources. Adults may be more apt to see the vigorous growth and determination of spirit in children; but in most cases, these aren't necessarily seen as positive characteristics. So to say children are strong and sturdy? Laughable, at the very least.

Which is why we adults, in our proud, strong and sturdy way, congratulate ourselves on our dedication to educate these young folks. With our superior strength, size, intellectual and spiritual resources, we will help the children in our lives to become like us. We will give them firm foundations from which to springboard into the rest of their lives. We will build them up in faith and character so they will one day build others up in a similar fashion.

Or will they do the same for us?

Yes, strong and sturdy is what we want our children to become; but strong and sturdy is also what our children are. Their determination to believe in the unseen, to live for their heart's one desire, to hold tenaciously to a concept, idea, or relationship is something most adults have lost the capacity to do. Their trusting, unpretentious, unquestioning faith drives their lives in a way adults can only dream about. Which is why, perhaps, Jesus says, "Let the little children come to Me, and do not hinder them, for the kingdom of heaven belongs to such as these" (Matthew 19:14).

By all means, teach the children in your midst, love them with all that you have, show by your life the love and grace of our Lord. But do not overlook what they may teach you, especially about faith and love and the simple joy of Christ. You may be surprised by the strength of their convictions and the sturdiness of their hand in yours, touching your heart.

Production Notes
Using Drama with Children

How do you use drama with children? How will they react? What is an appropriate response to drama in church? Who will direct? Who will act? Do the children have to memorize lines? What if I don't know the first thing about theater? If this is part of Sunday school or children's worship, what is the pastor's involvement? If you're just starting to use drama with children, you're probably asking some of these questions. We'd like to help you find the answers.

Drama and the Church

Drama has been a part of the church since Jesus' time. Take a look at the parables. Through them we see that Jesus wasn't a talking head. He realized people would better understand and retain what He told them if He spoke in word pictures. Drama is a natural extension of such word pictures. "Religious" drama re-creates and re-presents the amazing acts of God and His intercessions in human life. What better way to understand the passion of our Lord than through drama? What better way to understand our relationships with one another and with our Lord than through drama? Drama isn't "religious" merely because of its subject matter. Drama is religious when it arouses the audience's attention so they walk away with renewed spirits, exalted hearts, and a clearer understanding of God's work in their lives. Drama is religious when it forces us to confront our beliefs on the deepest spiritual level and, in that confrontation, to more clearly see ourselves in relation to our God.

That said, you have an awesome task. You have the privilege of using a tool that reaches and teaches the masses. You have the responsibility of making drama "religious." But how do you do that for *children*? Children have an amazing capacity for drama. They are often better than adults at the "willing suspension of disbelief" and are open to learning through drama because it gives them something "real" to grasp onto. Making drama "religious" for children is much more than using drama to tell Bible stories. It is using drama to teach children what the Bible stories mean—what lessons they hold for our lives. You'll find the dramas in this collection do just that. They don't all tell Bible stories but they all teach Bible lessons. As you use these dramas with your students, ask lots of questions: Why did the character do that? What did he mean when he said that? Has anything like this ever happened to you? Do you think this situation could really happen? You'll be surprised what you can learn from their answers.

So What Is Drama?

Drama for use in the church needs to meet the same criteria as drama for use in a theater:

1. It must have a point and make it.

2. The characters need to be realistic and believable (even in a farce, comedy, or reader's theater). They must be well-developed and convey realistic emotion.

3. The drama must have conflict. That doesn't mean that characters have to argue or fight; it means there must be a struggle between opposing forces—internal or external.

4. The drama must have a clear arc from beginning to middle to end. It must also have a clear climax. If the drama is to stand alone, it should have a clear resolution. There is a difference between resolution and conclusion. A resolution resolves the conflict; a conclusion brings a closing to the situation. If the drama is to be used as a sermon starter, it does not require a clear resolution of the conflict. The pastor will use the drama as a jumping-off point for his sermon; he will bring resolution to the conflict. If the drama is to be used in a children's church setting, the pastor or Sunday school teacher should follow the drama with a question and answer period or a brief message.

It's important that the drama have a point so it doesn't become mere entertainment during the worship service, Bible study, or Sunday school lesson. Drama, used correctly, can be an effective teaching tool. Used incorrectly it becomes a distraction.

Tips for Producing Drama

Most of the dramas in this book are brief enough to be used as *part* of a worship, devotional, or classroom setting. (Some are longer and can be used as a complete presentation.) Short dramas allow for minimal rehearsal and easy line memorization. Here are a few tips as you work with drama in your church.

1. *Let the drama serve the Word*. In most cases, especially when presented as part of a worship service, drama assists and enhances the reading and preaching of the Word. Each script in this collection includes at least one Scripture reference as well as questions for study and discussion and notes for the pastor or teacher. Dramas used to set up a sermon or children's message sometimes leave the audience begging for the Gospel message. At other times, the drama raises a question or evokes emotion or thought on a particular subject. In each instance, drama is an effective tool for teaching the Word of God: A pastor may choose to use a drama before, during, or after his sermon. A teacher may use drama to get students ready for the lesson. Or a drama can be used as a children's message, offering children a new way of understanding and responding to the Gospel. However it is used, it should enhance, not replace, the teaching of the Word.

2. *Recruit your actors.* If you're setting up a drama ministry in your church, it's best if your actors know something of the craft of acting. It may be difficult, but avoid asking for volunteers to serve as actors. Recruit people with a gift for and some experience in acting. That's not to say you can never use a novice. Sometimes they surprise you and, with a little extra coaching, can be effective members of the drama ministry. But most often, a team of volunteer actors who have never had any stage experience outside the annual Christmas pageant, doesn't make for an effective drama ministry. Compare your drama team to a church choir. Many church choirs are well-organized and have committed members who know something about music. So it should be with your drama ministry. Acting is a skill as is singing. The choir director doesn't allow just anyone to sing a solo—you should be as careful in selecting your actors. Likewise, the choir director is probably a trained musician. The drama director should be trained in his or her craft as well. Find someone in your congregation who has some professional theater experience or who has studied theater. His or her experience and training will add to the professionalism of your performances.

The dramas in this collection can be performed by children and for children (several have adults in the cast as well). Granted, you're not going to find many children in your church or Sunday school who have lots of acting experience, but they don't need it. Children are generally less inhibited than adults and that makes up for their lack of experience. Some of these dramas can be rehearsed by older children and performed for younger children. Some can be rehearsed by adults—teachers or your church's drama team—and performed for the children in a Sunday school or children's church setting. Either way, remember that these dramas are instructional tools and should be as "polished" as possible for the best learning.

3. *Rehearse.* Though many of the dramas here are brief, they still need rehearsal time. You can't hand out scripts on Saturday afternoon and expect a stellar performance on Sunday morning. Get scripts to the actors early enough so they have time to memorize their lines. Walk through the drama several times with scripts in hand, then come back and rehearse again after lines are memorized. Take time before rehearsal to go through the script yourself. Figure out what it is saying and decide how best to share that message with your audience. Use the purpose statement and theme for the script to guide your reflections. Go into the first rehearsal prepared with blocking ideas, a clear understanding of the subtext, and a knowledge of the script's arc from beginning to middle to end. The more prepared you are before the first rehearsal, the better the rehearsal and performance. Remember to be flexible. If an actor has another idea for blocking or is reading subtext differently than you are, talk about it and come to an agreement.

Again, working with children changes some of the rules. You'll likely be more concerned that the child can memorize his lines than that he knows their nuances. That's fine. These scripts aren't meant to be complex. But they are meant to be rehearsed.

4. *Strive for more than bathrobes and sandals.* The church expects excellence from its musicians and preachers; it should expect no less from its drama performances. Many of the dramas need little or no set but where a set is required, it should enhance the drama. Be realistic with costuming. Don't use bathrobes and sandals for biblical costumes. Plan ahead enough to have a committee of people (who know something about sewing and costuming) design and build realistic costumes. Work with the actors to develop characters and to understand the subtext in the script. If at all possible, use professional theatrical lighting. It can enhance a script tremendously. We understand that you may not have these things available, so the scripts work just fine without them. Throughout this book, theatrical terminology such as center stage, down left, stage right, etc. was used for consistency. If you are unfamiliar with these terms, have no fear—simply use the stage layout on the next page to help you. (Note: UR is upstage right, or, simply, up right. URC is up right center, and so on. All stage directions are from the actor's point of view as he faces the audience.) And remember that these dramas can be performed in a variety of settings: a classroom, the chancel, a multi-purpose room, etc. Adapt the stage directions to work in your own space.

5. *Work with the pastor or teacher* to incorporate the drama into the service or Sunday school lesson. If the drama is to be used in a church service, ask your pastor how he wants to incorporate it. Does he want to look at a drama you chose first and have one theme throughout the service, supported by the drama, his sermon, and the music? Does he want to give you a service theme and ask you to find a drama to match it? Does he want to look at a script first and write his sermon to go with it? These are all good options. Good communication with your pastor helps to incorporate drama as part of the worship experience. The same is true if the drama is to be used in children's church or a Sunday school setting. Work with the person in charge of the rest of the event to make it cohesive.

So you're ready to get started. Whether you're just getting your feet wet with using drama or you're ready to start a full-fledged drama ministry, it is our prayer that these dramas are useful tools as you teach God's mighty Word to children.

The Editors

```
                    UPSTAGE

              ┌─────┬─────┬─────┬─────┬─────┐
              │ UR  │ URC │ UC  │ ULC │ UL  │
              ├─────┼─────┼─────┼─────┼─────┤
  STAGE       │  R  │ RC  │  C  │ LC  │  L  │      STAGE
  RIGHT       ├─────┼─────┼─────┼─────┼─────┤      LEFT
              │ DR  │ DRC │ DC  │ DLC │ DL  │
              └─────┴─────┴─────┴─────┴─────┘

                   DOWNSTAGE


                    AUDIENCE
```

Production Notes
Using Sketches

Sketches are perhaps the easiest form of drama to use. They are often lighthearted and short which makes them fun to work on. They are frequently used to set up a sermon or message so they don't have to resolve any conflict. And they don't usually have any Gospel message on their own—it's supplied by the pastor in his message following the drama. But they require rehearsal all the same. Because sketches are short, there is less time to make the point. Actors need to be sharp and well-rehearsed.

You'll find that most of our sketches have small casts and require little or no set. The focus is not on the theatrics but on getting the message across. Let that be your focus as well as you prepare for performance. Work with the actors on blocking, characterization, line memorization, and timing. Discuss the message of the script with the cast so you're all telling the same story. Work with the pastor to determine what part the sketch plays in the service and how he plans to resolve the conflict or situation set up in the script.

Keep the performance simple so the message is clear.

Shadrach, Meshach, and Abednego

by Chad Hoover

Purpose: To help children learn the story of Shadrach, Meshach, and Abednego

Theme: Knowledge of God; trust in God

Scripture: Daniel 3

Time: 5–7 minutes

Cast: **King Nebuchadnezzar**—a very powerful, vain king

Herald—a confused gentleman

Shadrach—a believer in God

Meshach—a believer in God

Abednego—a believer in God

Flames—3–5 people to act as flames in a furnace

Angel

Person #1

Person #2

Soldier #1

Soldier #2

Crowd

Costumes: King wears distinguished-looking robes and a crown; Herald wears plain robes; Shadrach, Meshach, and Abednego are dressed alike, in plain robes; everyone else wears plain robes

Props: Throne-like chair; scroll

Lighting: General

Sound: No sound effects necessary

Setting: King Nebuchadnezzar's palace

Notes: Place the king's throne center stage; king will sit on it throughout the sketch. When the flames enter, they will "build" the furnace downstage right.

Shadrach, Meshach, and Abednego

by Chad Hoover

KING ENTERS and sits on throne with a flourish.

KING

(To audience) My name is Nebuchadnezzar! KING Nebuchadnezzar! I am very powerful. Everyone must do as I say ... or else!

HERALD

(ENTERS, bows before KING) O great Nebuchadoozle—

KING

That's Nebuchadnezzar, fool. Nebuchadnezzar.

HERALD

Nebuchadnezzar, right! *(Starting over again)* O great Nezzerbuchneb. Oh, shucks!

KING

It's *Nebuchadnezzar*! Why on earth is that so difficult?

HERALD

I'm sorry dear, sweet sir. Allow me to start all over again. *(Runs OFF and RE-ENTERS.)* O great ... King, what is thy bidding today?

KING

Why, I'm glad you asked, Herald! *(Secretly and proudly)* I have made an image of gold!

HERALD

No!?

KING

Yes! Yes!! It's 90 feet high and 9 feet wide. Very large—heh, heh, heh—and beautiful! I want you to call the governors, advisors, treasurers, judges, magistrates, and all the other provincial officials together and we will bow down and worship it!

HERALD

Oooh. Good idea, sir! *(Reading from scroll, very importantly. CROWD, including all actors except FLAMES, ENTERS and gathers reverently around KING.)* Attention! Attention, governors, advisors, treasurers, judges, magistrates, and all the officials of the land! The great King Needlezzahrufner—*(continues through KING's line)*

KING

Nebuchadnezzar.

HERALD

—summons you to bow down to the great big, monstrously huge, magnificently mammoth, extravagantly enlarged image of gold that King Zebboernflopter—*(continues through KING's line)*

KING

Nebuchadnezzar!

HERALD

—himself has set up, and worship it. You must do this because the great King Buzznerdachomper—*(continues through KING's line)*

KING

Nebuchadnezzar!!!

HERALD

—has commanded it. Whoever does not fall down and worship will immediately be thrown into a blazing furnace! *(Points downstage right. Three FLAMES ENTER and stand downstage right, slowly rotating in a small circle.)*

KING

Therefore, all you peoples, bow down to my beautiful image of gold.

Crowd bows down with the exception of SHADRACH, MESHACH, and ABEDNEGO. Everyone FREEZES unless speaking.

PERSON #1

(To SHADRACH, MESHACH, and ABEDNEGO) Hey! What are you doing? The king has ordered us to bow down and worship!

PERSON #2

He'll throw you into the fiery furnace if you do not obey him.

PERSON #1

You'll surely die in the furnace! There is no way you'll survive.

When SHADRACH, MESHACH, and ABEDNEGO speak, they continue each other's thoughts and words in smooth flowing verse.

SHADRACH

We're Shadrach,

MESHACH

Meshach,

ABEDNEGO

and Abednego!

SHADRACH

We serve the one God

MESHACH

the true God of Israel, and we will not bow down to King

ABEDNEGO

Nebuchadnezzar's idol.

SHADRACH

We have faith that our God

MESHACH

will save us from death.

ABEDNEGO

And even if He does not

SHADRACH

save us from death, we

MESHACH

still will not bow down.

ABEDNEGO

Not a chance!

Everyone UNFREEZES, but continues to bow. SHADRACH, MESHACH, and ABEDNEGO remain standing.

HERALD

O King! O King! Everybody is bowing down. This is gr— Uh oh! Um sir. There's, um, a problem. *(Tries to get KING's attention.)* Sir? King? Nebutahzeker? Magnadoodleeder? Nimblethemcookies? *(His voice raises as KING takes notice.)* They're not bowing down!

KING

(Still not quite understanding) They're what? Who?

HERALD

Shadrach, Meshach, and Abednego, sir! They're not bowing down.

KING

(Villainously) Bring them to me.

HERALD

At once, O Ne ... you kingly person! *(Crosses to SHADRACH, MESHACH, and ABED-NEGO.)* Shadrach, Meshach, and Abednego? Come with me! *(Leads them to KING. CROWD EXITS.)*

KING

(Speaking to the wrong actors) Is it true, Shadrach, Meshach, and Abednego?

ABEDNEGO

He's Shadrach!

MESHACH

I'm Meshach!

SHADRACH

And he's Abednego!

KING

(Not amused, nor caring) Oh? Well, is it true that you do not serve my gods or worship the image of gold I have set up?

SHADRACH

It is

MESHACH

true.

ABEDNEGO looks as if he's going to say something, but just nods in agreement.

KING

Then we have a problem, see, because you're supposed to do what I say! I will give you one more chance to bow down and worship the image I have made. If you do not worship it, you will be thrown immediately into a blazing furnace. Then what god will be able to save you from my hand?

SHADRACH

O Nebuchadnezzar,

MESHACH

we do not need to

ABEDNEGO

defend ourselves before you in this matter.

SHADRACH

If we are thrown into the blazing

MESHACH

furnace, the God we serve is able to save

ABEDNEGO

us from it, and He will rescue us from your

SHADRACH

hand, O King.

MESHACH

But even if He does not,

ABEDNEGO

we want you to

SHADRACH

know, O King,

MESHACH

that we will not serve

ABEDNEGO

your gods

SHADRACH

or worship the image

MESHACH

of gold

ABEDNEGO

you have set up.

KING

Very well. *(KING stares menacingly at SHADRACH, MESHACH, and ABEDNEGO.)* I am truly furious with you Shadrach, Meshach, and Abednego!

MESHACH

He's Shadrach!

SHADRACH

He's Meshach!

ABEDNEGO

And I'm Abednego!

KING

(Annoyed) Herald, have the furnace heated seven times hotter than usual.

HERALD

Wow! That would make it very, very, veeeeerrrrry hot! *(HERALD EXITS. He RE-ENTERS with more FLAMES, and they join the circle. FLAMES begin to rotate faster.)*

KING

I need the strongest soldiers in my army to come at once! *(Two SOLDIERS ENTER.)* Soldiers, take them and throw them into the blazing furnace!

SOLDIERS

As you wish, O wonderful King! *(SOLDIERS grab SHADRACH, MESHACH, and ABEDNEGO.)*

SOLDIER #1

(Crossing to furnace) Hmm ... it's a tad bit warm, this furnace!

SOLDIER #2

Yup. Let's open the door and just throw them in real quick!

SOLDIER #1

(They pantomime opening a door. The FLAMES separate to make an opening.) Whew! It's really hot now, huh!

SOLDIER #2

Sure is! Let's close the door before we—

FLAMES grab SOLDIERS, and pull them into their circle. SOLDIERS now become FLAMES. SHADRACH, MESCHACH, and ABEDNEGO step into the middle of them. FLAMES circle around them.

HERALD

Sir, the furnace was so hot that the flames of the fire killed the soldiers who took up Shadrach, Meshach, and Abednego! *(As HERALD says this, ANGEL ENTERS, and joins SHADRACH, MESHACH, and ABEDNEGO in the furnace.)*

KING

(Jumping to his feet) Wait a minute! Weren't there three men that we tied up and threw into the fire?

HERALD

(Counting on his fingers) Certainly, O King!

KING

But look! I see four men walking around in the fire, unbound and unharmed, and the fourth looks like a son of gods. *(Shouts into furnace)* Shadrach, Meshach, and Abednego, servants of the Most High God, come out! Come here!

SHADRACH

Shall we?

MESHACH

After you!

ABEDNEGO

(Shaking ANGEL's hand) Thank you!

SHADRACH, MESHACH, and ABEDNEGO EXIT *the furnace.*

HERALD

King Nebloncadeezar! The fire has not harmed their bodies, nor is a hair on their heads singed; their clothes are not scorched, and there is no smell of fire on them!

KING

Praise be to the God of Shadrach, Meshach, and Abednego, who has sent His angel and rescued His servants! They trusted Him and defied the king's command and were willing to give their lives rather than serve or worship any god except their own. No other god can save this way!

SHADRACH

Thanks be

MESHACH

to God!

ABEDNEGO looks as if he's going to say something, but instead just nods in agreement. ALL EXIT together.

Shadrach, Meshach, and Abednego

by Chad Hoover

A Note to the Pastor or Teacher:

Just the right length for a children's message, this sketch teaches children a beautiful piece of history from the Bible. The word "image" may be unfamiliar to young children; "statue" could be substituted. Also, we suggest placing some kind of idol or image on stage as the lack of one could be misleading to children who see their parents kneel down and pray to their God who is unseen. This problem is easily solved by a carefully placed prop.

This sketch can be used as a catechetical tool to teach the "second" commandment: "You will not make for yourself an idol ... nor worship them. As Martin Luther says in his explanation to the first commandment, "Idolatry does not consist merely of erecting an image and praying to it. It is primarily in the heart." Important to emphasize here is the concept that trust in God is not a faith that is headstrong and without foundation. Rather, Shadrach, Meshach, and Abednego knew God, knew His Word, and through faith trusted in Him in the face of certain death. This lesson in faith is relevant today and in every age as Christians face persecution, torture, and death because they believe, teach, and confess Jesus as Lord and Savior.

Questions for Study and Discussion:

1. Why did Shadrach, Meshach, and Abednego disobey King Nebuchadnezzar?
2. What do you think these three men were feeling both before and after they fell into the fiery furnace?
3. When do you have a chance to tell people what you believe about Jesus?
4. Look at Isaiah 43:1–5a. What promises and reassurances do you find there?

Strong and Sturdy

by Lisa Gaylord

Purpose: To help children learn that the Word of God makes a Christian strong and sturdy in the face of temptation and spiritual danger

Theme: Word of God; confidence; fear

Scripture: Matthew 7:24–27

Time: 7–10 minutes

Cast: **Narrator**

Wolf

Frankfurter—a pig with a German accent

Wilbur—a pig with a western accent

Hamlet—a studious, well-meaning pig

Costumes: Actors wear contemporary clothing and animal noses

Props: 3 Bibles; 1 large storybook; 1 tall stool; 1 large chair, such as a recliner; end table

Lighting: General

Sound: No sound effects necessary

Setting: The pigs' homes

Notes: The stool is set downstage right; the chair is set stage left, facing the TV, with the end table next to the chair. The Bible and remote control sit on the table.

Strong and Sturdy

by Lisa Gaylord

NARRATOR ENTERS, carrying the storybook, and sits on stool.

NARRATOR

Our story begins like any good story does: Once upon a time, there were three little pigs. Their Sunday school teacher taught them to build their lives on a firm foundation, just like Jesus said. A firm foundation is something strong and solid, so their teacher told them to build their lives on the love and grace of Jesus. Learning God's Word would help them remember they had this firm foundation of faith, and would help them build upon it. That way, when bad things came into their lives, like problems, troubles, their own sins, or *(whispers and looks around)* even the big bad wolf, they would stay strong and sturdy. *(NARRATOR opens the book. FRANKFURTER ENTERS. He yawns and stretches lazily.)* So the three little pigs set out to build on that firm foundation. The first little pig, Frankfurter, was a lazy little pig. If there was a chance to do something the easy way, Frankfurter would eventually get around to it.

FRANKFURTER

Yah! Mine little eyes, zey alvays vant to cloze. And mine little pigsfeet, zey get tired, zo fast! *(He flops down into chair, then spots the Bible.)* Ach du lieber, I better get working on zat foundation. *(He picks up and then puts down the Bible.)* But I feel a little znooze comink on. *(He slouches down on his chair, just skimming his Bible on his lap and not even looking at it.)*

NARRATOR

So, Frankfurter was working on his ever-so-easy but ever-so-sloppy and ever-so-flimsy foundation when trouble came to his door.

WOLF ENTERS.

WOLF

(Growling to NARRATOR) Trouble?!

NARRATOR

(Gulps and clears his throat) Excuse me, Mr. Wolf, but I'm just reading what the script says.

WOLF reads over NARRATOR's shoulder. FRANKFURTER reacts to WOLF's presence.

WOLF

"... ever-so-flimsy foundation when trouble came to his door." Trouble? No, no, no, no! I just wanted to ask my dear friend, Frankfurter, over for dinner tonight. In fact, I want him to be the guest of honor. Yeah, me and a few close friends, we're having a pigroast! Ha-Ha-Ha-Ha-Ha!

FRANKFURTER

Ze pigroast. How nize! Ze guest of honor! *(Does a double take)* Ze guest of honor?! Ach du lieber!

NARRATOR

Frankfurter knew that he was in big trouble.

FRANKFURTER

Yah! Ze great big trouble.

WOLF

Little piggie, little piggie, come on snout here!

NARRATOR

Come on snout here?

WOLF

You got a problem with that?

NARRATOR

(Nervously) The wolf said—

WOLF

Little piggie, little piggie, come on snout here!

NARRATOR

And the little pig remembered that their beloved teacher had told him the Word of God helps remind him of his firm foundation in Jesus, and he'd be able to get through any kind of trouble. So he quoted a verse from the Bible.

WOLF

The Bible!

The NARRATOR and WOLF wait, but FRANKFURTER just stands there trying to remember.

NARRATOR

The little pig quoted a verse from the Bible. *(Pause)* Frankfurter?

FRANKFURTER

Jesus vept!?!

NARRATOR AND WOLF

Jesus wept?

FRANKFURTER

Yah, it's za only verse dat was easy to learn.

NARRATOR

Well, I'm sad to say, that Frankfurter had not learned anything from Scripture and now the wolf was at his door! And the wolf huffed and he …

WOLF

(To Narrator) Do you mind? *(To Frankfurter)* I'll huff and I'll puff and I'm coming in!

NARRATOR

Okay. So he huffed and he puffed and he blew the pig down. In fact, Frankfurter's foundation was so flimsy that *I* could have blown it down. But when the dust cleared, the wolf searched the house for the pig—

FRANKFURTER EXITS.

WOLF

Hey, where'd he go?

NARRATOR

The wolf couldn't find the piggie. Frankfurter had barely escaped with his life.

WOLF

No problem, I'll find him later. It'll be easy now that I know he can't keep me away. I'll go after his friend. I can see his house. *(WOLF EXITS.)*

NARRATOR

Now, our second little pig is Wilbur. *(WILBUR ENTERS.)* Wilbur knows he should build up his foundation to be strong and sturdy.

WILBUR

Ah, yep! Da Sunday school teacher said—strong and sturdy. Strong and sturdy. Yep. *(Sits in chair.)*

NARRATOR

The only problem is that Wilbur is very easily distracted. Anything can steal his concentration.

WILBUR

Yep. And I have a hard time keeping my mind on things too. *(WILBUR picks up the Bible and then notices the TV. He puts down the Bible and picks up the remote control.)*

NARRATOR

Uh, yeah. Well, Wilbur built his foundation in between playing video games, blowing bubbles, talking to his friends, watching re-runs of the Brady Bunch ...

WILBUR

I just love this show!

NARRATOR

And of course—eating.

WILBUR

Yep! I'm just a little piggie.

NARRATOR

He was all cozy in his dirty little house when a great big problem arrived at his doorstep.

WOLF

(To NARRATOR) A problem?

NARRATOR

The script says—

WOLF

I know. I know. A great big problem. Well, shows how much you know. I was going to have a little brunch for some of my friends and I wanted to invite old Wilbur here. We're going to have some pigs-in-a-blanket. Ha-Ha-Ha! Little piggie! Little piggie! Get snout here!

WILBUR

Well, I'll be hog-tied, it's the wolf!

NARRATOR

Now, Wilbur remembered that a strong foundation would help him deal with the wolf just like his teacher taught him.

WILBUR

Well, Gow-owly! Let's see here. I gotta study on this here a spell.

WOLF smacks his lips and rubs his hands together.

NARRATOR

Oh, dear!

WILBUR

I think it's in Romans somewheres.

NARRATOR

Don't you know?

WILBUR

Well, you know, I meant to study on it. I've been meaning to sorta soak it in an' let it work in me to make me strong and sturdy, just like my teacher said, but, golly, I've been kinda busy.

WOLF

Good. I'll huff and I'll puff and here I come!

WILBUR EXITS.

NARRATOR

So, he huffed and he puffed and he went in, but by the time he looked through the clutter, Wilbur had gone out the back door. It was a narrow escape!

WOLF

Never mind! I know where another one lives. I'll get this piggie later on.

NARRATOR

Now the last little pig was a very smart little pig named Hamlet.

HAMLET

(HAMLET ENTERS.) To build or not to build, that is the question. *(He sits in the chair.)*

NARRATOR

And Hamlet knew the right answer. He knew his Sunday school teacher was right. He needed to keep building his life on a firm foundation. So, he studied God's Word and learned more and more about what God had done for him—things that would really keep him strong in the face of danger.

HAMLET

(Holds Bible but concentrates as if remembering) Let's see here. I need a firm foundation. Hmm.

NARRATOR

Hamlet studied long and hard and prayed long and hard, and after time, he had a strong and beautiful foundation of faith in God. Then one day, he was sitting by his cozy fire, *(WOLF ENTERS)* when there was a knock at the door. It was *(WOLF glares at the NARRATOR)* ... a wolf. It was a wolf.

WOLF

Hey pig. Open up. I'm getting tired of all this. I'm having a barbeque and without you, all I got is sauce.

NARRATOR

But Hamlet stood unafraid on his solid foundation and said—

HAMLET

Excuse me, Mr. Wolf. 1 John 5:14 says, "Now this is the confidence that we have in Him"—that's Jesus, Mr. Wolf—*(WOLF cowers)* "that if we ask anything according to His will, He hears us." And Mr. Wolf? I think I know what He thinks about you trying to make porkchops out of me 'cause in John 10:28–29, Jesus says, "And I give them eternal life, and they shall never perish; neither shall anyone snatch them out of My hand. My Father, who has given them to Me, is greater than all; *(WOLF slinks OFF)* and no one is able to snatch them out of My Father's hand." So, you see, I can resist you with confidence. I know the truth. Mr. Wolf? Mr. Wolf? Hmm. He must have gone. Oh, well, back to studying. *(Takes Bible and EXITS.)*

NARRATOR

So the trouble, that great big problem, that wolf, could not huff and puff his way through a firm foundation. *(WOLF ENTERS, hands on hips listening to NARRATOR.)* He couldn't even face it! He went away less sure of himself, pretty hungry, and worried about all those other hungry people he invited over for dinner. The big bad wolf was beaten by a little pig.

WOLF

I could always serve roast storyteller.

NARRATOR

Watch it—I have a firm foundation too!

WOLF

Curses! Foiled again! *(EXITS)*

NARRATOR

Well, as for the three little pigs: Hamlet helped Wilbur and Frankfurter study the Bible. And they all learned how to let God's Word teach them how much God loves them and keeps them strong. Now they all would be ready the next time anything big and bad came to their door. And with God's help, they all lived strong and sturdy ever after. The End. *(NARRATOR closes the book and EXITS.)*

Strong and Sturdy

by Lisa Gaylord

A Note to the Pastor or Teacher:

Well suited for a chapel setting, "Strong and Sturdy" plays on the feelings of fear and confidence. The wolf has confidence in his ability to overcome the pigs but it is a false confidence in the face of the greater power of the Word of God. The pigs fear for their lives because they had a false confidence in their ability to remember the promises of God in times of need.

Confidence and fear are emotions given by God for our benefit. Fear can warn us when we are in danger (see Psalm 27:1–3) and confidence can encourage our brothers and sisters in Christ (see Phillipians 3:1–7). The Word of God brings confidence greater than fear because it creates the faith which believes Christ died and rose again and has defeated the devil, the world, and our sinful flesh.

Memorization of the Word is neither a "cure-all" nor a "switch." The Word is the foundation of truth, as Hamlet says, and the Word is an activity that requires the time Wilbur wasted on other trivial matters. Continuing study of God's Word builds a relationship between our Creator God and us, His adopted children in Christ. When temptations and trials assail us, we can stand on the promises we have learned and trust in. And when we succumb to temptations and trials, we can fall into the arms of our loving and gracious God who forgives His children on account of His Son Jesus.

Questions for Study and Discussion:

1. What kinds of temptations and trials (like the wolf) attack your faith in Jesus?

2. Who are the Christians in your life to whom you can go when you are having trouble finding places in God's Word that address your temptations and trials?

3. How could you help your friends who act like Frankfurter and Wilbur?

4. How does Baptism begin to create the firm foundation believers have in Christ?

Giving God Glory

by Cheryl Kirking

Purpose: To demonstrate ways to give God glory

Theme: Christian living

Scripture: 1 John 3:16–20; 1 Corinthians 10:31

Time: 3–5 minutes

Cast: **Jordan**—adult man or woman

Grady—age 9

Costumes: Contemporary clothing appropriate for character

Props: A bench or several chairs; book; Rollerblades

Lighting: General

Sound: No sound effects necessary

Setting: A park

Giving God Glory

by Cheryl Kirking

JORDAN is sitting on the bench, center stage, reading. GRADY ENTERS, rollerblading, or carrying the skates.

JORDAN

Hi Grady! How are you?

GRADY

Oh, hi, Miss Jordan. I saw you this morning at church, but I didn't have time to say hi. I didn't want to be late for Sunday school.

JORDAN

Oh, that's okay. How was Sunday school today?

GRADY

It was okay. My teacher, Mrs. Miller, is really old, but I like her. She wears those weird chain things on her glasses, but otherwise she's pretty cool. Sometimes she says things I don't really understand—like today she said God wants us to give Him all we have. But I don't get it. I mean, what would God want with my Rollerblades?

JORDAN

Hmm, good question. But would you be willing to give them to Him, if He wanted them?

GRADY

Well, I suppose I would—I mean if God asked for them. *(Pauses, alarmed)* Do you think He might?!?

JORDAN

Well, I think—

GRADY

(Interrupting, even more alarmed) How about my Gameboy?

JORDAN

Well, I don't think that's really—

GRADY

(Interrupting again, very alarmed) Not my new official soccer ball?!?

JORDAN

Well, let me put it this way. God wants us to glorify Him in all we do. Can you think of a way that you can glorify God with that new soccer ball?

GRADY

Huh?

JORDAN

How could you use that soccer ball to show people God's love?

GRADY

I could write "Jesus loves you" all over it!

JORDAN

Yes, you could. But those are just words. I think God is looking more for actions than just words. For example, when we are kind to others, we are showing God's love and that glorifies God.

GRADY

So what's that got to do with my new soccer ball? *(He pauses to think for a moment)* Oh, hey—I could *share* my new soccer ball! Yeah! And I could help my little sister learn how to kick it. She's always bugging me to teach her how.

JORDAN

I like that idea. How do you think your sister would feel?

GRADY

Happy, I guess.

JORDAN

I think God would be happy too, because you are sharing love and kindness.

GRADY

Oh I get it. That's how I could use my soccer ball to ... to ... gl-glor-glor ... What you said.

JORDAN

Glorify God.

GRADY

Yeah, I could use my soccer ball to glorify God.

JORDAN

That's what it means to give God all we have, to be willing to use all we have and all we are, to serve Him.

GRADY

Hmm. I kind of understand, but I'll have to think about that some more. Maybe when I'm playing soccer.

JORDAN

Good idea. I'll see you later, okay?

GRADY

Okay, Miss Jordan. Bye! *(He EXITS.)*

JORDAN

Bye!

After a moment, she EXITS.

Giving God Glory

by Cheryl Kirking

A Note to the Pastor or Teacher:

This sketch is a succinct lead-in for a discussion about life in the kingdom of God beginning early and continuing throughout life. Demonstrating what 1 John 3:18 means, this "teaser" doesn't explain verse 16 of the same chapter but it is this verse which truly shows us what it means to give God all we have, to be willing to use all we have and all we are to serve Him.

Christian living is first a question of control. Who is in control of your life? Is Jesus in control or are you? As Christ lives in us, our bodies are dead in sin and the Spirit is life (see Romans 8:10). The faithful taking up of our cross will lead to more than saying "Jesus loves you" and sharing soccer balls but we need to start somewhere.

And Christian living is also a question of eschatology, for a person would only be "foolish" enough to give up his life if he believed in an eternal hope. This hope of life which never ends in the presence and glory of God forms and informs every action of the Christian, beginning in the waters of Baptism.

Questions for Study and Discussion:

1. Who are some adults to whom you can go when you have questions about God and His involvement in your life?

2. How can Miss Jordan serve and glorify God? (Hint: She did these things in the sketch—can you identify how?)

3. Can our actions win favor with God? If not, why do we act in ways that glorify God?

4. How did Jesus make God happy? (Hint: See the account of Jesus' Baptism in the Bible.)

Production Notes:
Using Full-length Plays and Programs

Rehearse. Rehearse. Rehearse. Full-length plays and programs can be dynamic ministry tools but they require some work. You'll need help. Don't try to organize a full-length program by yourself. At the least, you'll need a director and a producer. The director's focus is on working with the actors during the rehearsal process to bring the script to life. The producer's job is to oversee musicians and crews working on props, costumes, set, and lighting. As with any drama, the director should have studied the script and have a vision for the performance. It is his or her job to help the actors realize that vision. It is up to the producer to help the costumer and other designers work with that vision as well. If the director tries to function as both director and producer, he or she will lose focus on the script and the performance will show it. A producer doesn't necessarily need theater experience; he or she needs to be well organized and energetic.

In a full-length script, costumes, set, and lighting become more important. They actually help to tell the story. It may be more difficult to find professionals to help you with these areas but look for people with at least some experience. For example, a good seamstress will have experience "building" clothing. She could be helpful in costuming. An art teacher could be helpful in designing a set while a shop teacher could be in charge of building it.

As you set up your rehearsal process, don't try to rehearse the entire script at every rehearsal. Break it up into scenes or beats and rehearse only one or two of these at a time. When you've rehearsed each scene or beat several times, put the whole thing together for a rehearsal called a run-through. During the run-through, evaluate which individual scenes need more work and call additional rehearsals for those scenes. Have at least one or two full run-throughs before the actual performance. The week before the performance in a theater is called "tech week." It is during this week that all technical aspects of the show from costumes and makeup to sets and lighting come together. During this week, have at least one run-through that includes all aspects of the performance. Don't allow actors to stop during this run-through. Treat it as a performance. This allows actors to experience the entire show without a break as they will during the actual performance. It allows you to see what the entire show looks like from beginning to end without stopping. This run-through will tell you if you're ready for an audience.

If the script is to be used as part of a worship service, work with the pastor to make the entire service cohesive. If the script is a performance on its own, separate from a worship setting, make sure the audience has a message to take home with them. Keep your actors focused on what that message is and how they are helping to spread it.

What's a Nice Jewish Girl Like You Doing in a Persian Harem?

by Barbara Hollenbach

Purpose: To teach children the story of Esther

Theme: Heroes for today

Scripture: The book of Esther

Time: 45–60 minutes

Cast: **Young Esther**—age 8–10; contemporary girl

Grandma—age 60+; Young Esther's grandmother; contemporary

King Xerxes—ruler of Persia

Harbona—personal servant to King Xerxes

Vashti—queen of Persia

Memucan—advisor to King Xerxes

Mordecai—cousin to Esther; advisor to King Xerxes; Jew

Esther—cousin to Mordecai; becomes Xerxes' queen; Jew

Hathach—personal servant to Queen Esther

Bigthana—plots to kill King Xerxes

Teresh—plots to kill King Xerxes

Haman—trusted advisor of King Xerxes; a bit full of himself

Zeresh—Haman's wife

Esther's Servant Girl

Esther's Male Servant

Town Crier

6 Advisors

3 Friends of Haman

6 Servants—extras

Persian Men—extras

Persian Women—extras

3 Listeners—extras

Chorus

Costumes: Biblically accurate clothing

Props: Cups and plates for parties; scroll; change of clothing for Mordecai; golden scepter; ring (King Xerxes)

Sound: No sound effects necessary

Setting: King Xerxes' palace

Notes: For performance, be sure to play on the comedic elements inherent in the script. Hathach is a fun, broadly drawn character and the songs are lively and funny. The cast is large, so rehearsals may be challenging. It is helpful to rehearse the chorus separately and to rehearse the play in three parts, dividing at Bigthana's entrance and again at Esther's line "So I look alright?" Then bring the parts together to rehearse the whole play. If you have a small group, feel free to double up on minor roles. Chorus members may play minor roles as well.

What's a Nice Jewish Girl Like You Doing in a Persian Harem?

by Barbara Hollenbach

YOUNG ESTHER and GRANDMA ENTER and cross downstage right.

YOUNG ESTHER

I'm really glad you came to visit, Grandma. I've missed you a lot.

GRANDMA

I've missed you too, Esther.

They hug each other and sit down.

YOUNG ESTHER

You know, David told me yesterday that he was named after a famous king of Israel, who won lots of battles and wrote lots of songs. He sounds like a really cool person to be named after.

GRANDMA

Well, Esther, you were named after someone too. Even though she never fought in a battle, she was a real hero.

YOUNG ESTHER

A hero named Esther? Cool! Please tell me about her.

GRANDMA

Well, she lived in a country called Persia more than 2,000 years ago. Back then in Persia, women weren't allowed to do very much. But one woman managed to save thousands of lives. Do you want to hear about her?

YOUNG ESTHER

Well, maybe, but the one I really want to hear about is Esther.

GRANDMA

(Laughing) You will. Listen to this story.

XERXES, MORDECAI, ESTHER, and HAMAN ENTER and move downstage center. They speak to the audience, but react to one another.

XERXES

I am King Xerxes of Persia. I am rich and powerful, even though people tell me I don't always act very smart.

MORDECAI

I am Mordecai, the Jew. I have to walk a very fine line to follow the customs of my people and yet survive in Persia, where my people are not always loved.

ESTHER

I am Esther, a Jewish girl. I am pretty, but I know it takes more than good looks to get along in life.

HAMAN

I am Haman the Agagite. I am conceited and ambitious and I hate Jews. I am also a good con man *(aside)* and I've tricked King Xerxes into doing things my way so many times—and he doesn't even know!

ESTHER and MORDECAI EXIT. XERXES and HAMAN move upstage to get settled for the party. CHORUS and HARBONA ENTER and gather around XERXES. CHORUS remains standing as they sing. All songs about XERXES are sung to the tune of "Zacchaeus;" phrases enclosed in double slashes are repeated.

CHORUS

King Xerxes was a very rich man, a very rich man was he.

He wanted to show off his wealth so all his friends could see.

He gave a party for his friends that lasted days and days.

He wanted them to see his wealth //and give him lots of praise.//

He served them wine, and then some more; they really drank it up.

The king got drunk and then he bragged as he drained another cup.

He said his queen was a gorgeous chick, and then he acted dumb.

He sent a servant to the queen //and ordered her to come.//

CHORUS sits with XERXES. VASHTI and PERSIAN WOMEN ENTER right and sit, talking quietly. Men are drinking and talking.

XERXES

(Slurring) Well, gentlemen, I hope you are enjoying my party. If anyone needs more wine, just say the word, and my servants will fill your cups. There's no lack here at King Xerxes' palace, no, no, no. *(Pauses, taking a big drink from his cup.)* And no lack of beautiful women either. In fact, I say that Vashti, my queen, is the most beautiful woman in all of Persia. And if you don't believe it, I'll prove it to you. Servants!

HARBONA and two CHORUS members stand.

HARBONA

Yes, your majesty?

XERXES

Go to Queen Vashti's quarters, and tell her that I want her to put on her most beautiful robe and to come here right away so that everyone can see how beautiful she is.

HARBONA

Yes, your majesty.

HARBONA and other SERVANTS cross to VASHTI's party.

HARBONA

Queen Vashti, your majesty, King Xerxes is asking for you. He says to put on your most gorgeous robe and to go to his party. He has told everyone that you are the most beautiful woman in Persia, and he wants to prove it.

VASHTI

That party has been going on for a week. I'll bet he's had too much to drink, hasn't he?

HARBONA

I'm afraid so, your majesty.

VASHTI

Well, you go back and tell him that I am Queen Vashti of Persia, and I'm not going to parade myself in front of his drunken friends!

HARBONA

Are you sure you want me to tell him that? He'll be furious.

VASHTI

Yes! I'll risk it.

HARBONA and other SERVANTS return to XERXES' party.

HARBONA

Your majesty, I have done what you commanded, but Queen Vashti refuses to come.

XERXES

(Standing, furious) What? She's making a fool out of me in front of all these people! We'll see about this.

XERXES and party EXIT. VASHTI and party EXIT. CHORUS remains center stage.

CHORUS

King Xerxes was an angry man, and very bitter too.

His advisors came in when he called //to talk about what to do.//

XERXES and MEMUCAN ENTER, crossing downstage to join CHORUS. XERXES paces in front of them during his line.

XERXES

Gentlemen, we have a problem. Queen Vashti has disobeyed me. What is the best way to handle this?

MEMUCAN

(*Stepping forward slightly*) Your majesty, Queen Vashti has embarrassed you in front of your people. All the women of Persia will hear about this and refuse to obey their husbands. They will say, "If Queen Vashti can get away with it, so can we." So we need to write a new law, a law of the Medes and Persians that can never ever be changed. This law should say that Queen Vashti will no longer be queen because of what she has done. When the women in your great kingdom hear about this, they'll respect their husbands.

XERXES

(*Stops pacing, smiles*) Thus have you suggested; thus shall it be done! Write a letter about this and send it to all parts of my kingdom!

MEMUCAN

Yes, your majesty.

MEMUCAN EXITS. XERXES and CHORUS cross upstage. PERSIAN WOMEN and other EXTRAS ENTER. TOWN CRIER ENTERS, crossing down center.

TOWN CRIER

(*Reading from scroll*) Since Queen Vashti refused to obey her husband, let it be known that she is no longer queen. Let it further be known that all women must obey their husbands, and all children must obey their fathers.

PERSIAN MEN and WOMEN are listening; MEN look pleased, and WOMEN look upset and scared. They FREEZE during GRANDMA's lines.

YOUNG ESTHER

I don't think I would have liked living in Persia back then.

GRANDMA

No, you probably wouldn't. But you know what? Esther lived there, and even though she was treated that way, she still managed to be a hero. Listen!

CROWD EXITS. XERXES sits forlornly center stage; MEMUCAN and HARBONA are near him. CHORUS gathers around him as well.

CHORUS

Now King Xerxes had no queen; he was a lonely man.

His counselors told him not to fret; //they'd come up with a plan.//

CHORUS sits around XERXES.

XERXES

I really miss Queen Vashti. I sort of wish I hadn't gotten so drunk. But what's done is done. *(Sighs)*

MEMUCAN

With all due respect, your majesty, you need to remember that there's more than one pebble on the beach. There are lots of beautiful young women in Persia. You're the king—you can have any girl you want. You should have your officers find a whole lot of them and bring them here. Then you can choose the one you like best to be the new queen.

XERXES

(Smiles) Thus has it been spoken; thus shall it be done. Go and give the order!

XERXES and MEMUCAN EXIT. CHORUS stands downstage left. All songs about MORDECAI are sung to the tune of "Chief of Sinners Though I Be."

CHORUS

Mordecai was kind and good,
Always did the things he should.
He wasn't quite a Persian true,
'Cause, you see, he was a Jew.
Kept the customs of his race,

Lived in Persia by wits and grace.

His cousin Esther was orphaned there;

He took her in and gave her care.

Taught her well, she kept his rules;

She turned out to be quite cool.

Not just smart; but pretty too,

and Xerxes' scouts said, "We want you."

MORDECAI and ESTHER ENTER.

MORDECAI

Well, cousin Esther, you leave tomorrow morning. As soon as I heard about King Xerxes' search for a new queen, I knew they would choose you to be one of the contestants. I'm not sure I like it very much, but there's nothing I can do about it. You're very pretty, you know.

ESTHER

Thank you, Mordecai. You've always been so kind. It's hard to imagine I'll never see you again once I'm inside King Xerxes' harem.

MORDECAI

(Stops walking and turns ESTHER to face him.) Esther, it's an advantage for a girl to be pretty, but there are some things that are even more important. You need to realize that a king's palace is full of problems, and you need to play it cool—very cool. Keep your eyes open and your mouth shut. Don't tell everything you know. For example, our family is Jewish, and not everyone in Persia loves Jews. So if I were you, I wouldn't tell anyone that you are a Jew. Not that you should forget your people—not at all! It's really important for you to remember everything I've taught you about how to live right and how to get along. But keep your mouth sealed, okay?

ESTHER

Don't worry. I'll remember all you told me. Good night, Mordecai.

MORDECAI EXITS. ESTHER sits. During song, XERXES ENTERS and walks around ESTHER, nodding and smiling.

CHORUS

King Xerxes looked at all the girls; he didn't need a shove.

He took one look at Esther's face, and then he fell in love.

He made her queen, gave her a crown, and said, "Let's celebrate!"

He threw a party, and his friends //all drank and drank and ate.//

XERXES EXITS. All songs about ESTHER are sung to the tune of "Puff the Magic Dragon." Italicized questions at the ends of verses are spoken.

CHORUS

(Gathering around ESTHER) Esther won the contest; she became the queen.

She was the prettiest girl King Xerxes' eyes had ever seen.

She was kind and pleasant, and people liked her ways.

She charmed the Persian palace, and she won lots of praise.

(To ESTHER) But, Esther, what's a nice Jewish girl like you doing in a Persian harem? (ESTHER shrugs.)

One reason she could cope was that her cousin raised her right.

She never got in trouble; she behaved both day and night.

She kept her word to Mordecai, never broke his rules,

Never told them she was Jewish, really played it cool.

(To ESTHER) But Esther, what IS a nice Jewish girl like you doing in a Persian harem? (ESTHER shrugs again and EXITS.)

CHORUS

King Xerxes was a party king; he liked wine, women, and song.

So he needed help to rule the land, or things would go quite wrong.

He quickly saw that Mordecai was cool and wise and fine;

So he had him work at the palace gate //so he could drink more wine.//

XERXES and MORDECAI ENTER. XERXES gestures grandly upstage, as if showing the palace gate. MORDECAI shakes his hand, then walks upstage to take up his post. XERXES EXITS.

CHORUS

Mordecai sat at the gate;

He treated people fair and straight.

Did good things that all could see;

It's what we call integrity.

He spoke the truth for all to hear,

Then slept at night, his conscience clear.

MORDECAI paces. After a moment, BIGTHANA and TERESH ENTER. They look around to make sure no one has followed them. They don't see MORDECAI.

BIGTHANA

(In stage whisper) Teresh, I am so mad at King Xerxes.

TERESH

Me too. I know—let's kill him!

MORDECAI stops walking, hides, and listens.

BIGTHANA

Think we could get away with it?

TERESH

Yeah. I have an idea how we could do it. *(Whispers)*

BIGTHANA

I think it will work. Let's go!

BIGTHANA and TERESH EXIT. MORDECAI steps out of hiding. HATHACH ENTERS.

MORDECAI

Ah, Hathach, am I glad to see you. How is the honorable Queen Esther today?

HATHACH

Very well, thank you. And how are you, officer Mordecai?

MORDECAI

I am well, but I have a message of great urgency for his majesty, King Xerxes, and I think the best way to get it to him is through Queen Esther. Can you give her a message for me?

HATHACH

Yes, your honor.

MORDECAI

Go and tell Queen Esther there is a plot against her husband's life and she needs to warn him! She can get further details from me.

HATHACH

Yes, your honor. *(Bows and EXITS.)*

MORDECAI continues to stand in front of the gate, upstage. XERXES and MEMUCAN ENTER and cross downstage during line. CHORUS gathers around them.

XERXES

Well, it's a good thing that Mordecai overheard Bigthana and Teresh's plans to kill me. Thanks to him I'm alive, and those two scoundrels are dead instead. Memucan, write all this in the annals of my kingdom right now!

MEMUCAN

Yes, your highness.

XERXES keeps walking and EXITS. MEMUCAN writes feverishly. CHORUS steps away from him during the next song.

All songs about HAMAN are sung to the tune of "Reuben Reuben, I've Been Thinking."

CHORUS

Haman, Haman so ambitious, shows up at the palace now.

Wants to be the top official and make all his rivals bow.

Haman is a real smooth talker; I don't trust that guy at all.

Xerxes, watch out for this scoundrel; he'll be sure to make you fall.

Haman, Haman got King Xerxes in the palm of Haman's hand.

Dull King Xerxes sure was snookered; and gave in to each demand.

He made Haman top official; all the others in the land

Had to bow in Haman's presence to obey the king's command.

MORDECAI, MEMUCAN, and CHORUS are standing at the gate. HAMAN ENTERS.

MEMUCAN

Hey, here comes Haman. We all have to kneel to him. That's what King Xerxes ordered.

HAMAN crosses to gate. Everyone kneels but MORDECAI, who slips to the back. HAMAN does not notice MORDECAI. HAMAN smiles smugly at those who kneel. Everyone gets up after he passes.

MEMUCAN

Hey, Mordecai, why didn't you kneel?

MORDECAI

I didn't kneel because I am a Jew. It's against the law I follow to worship any man. *(EXITS.)*

MEMUCAN

Hey, let's tell Haman that Mordecai didn't kneel and see if he gets on Mordecai's case about it.

CHORUS

Haman, Haman, heard about it, and he hated Mordecai.

He was angry, oh so angry, and he wanted him to die.

But it wasn't quite sufficient just to kill a single Jew.

Genocide is more efficient; let's kill all the others too.

First we'll settle on a time frame; we'll decide by casting lots.

When the day has been decided, we will make our clever plots.

I'll think of something to tell Xerxes to make him distrust the Jews,

And he'll agree to let me kill them when he hears my phony news.

XERXES ENTERS and grandly sits on his throne.

XERXES

(Muttering to himself) Now for my next party, what foods and wines shall I serve?

XERXES notices HAMAN and beckons to him.

XERXES

Ahh, Haman, my good man, what brings you here?

HAMAN

(Unctuously) Your majesty, there is a certain people living throughout your kingdom who do not follow the same customs we Persians do. Why, they don't even obey the king's laws. You know, your majesty—may you live forever—I don't think it is good for your kingdom to tolerate these people any longer. I've thought of a plan. If you like it, your majesty, let a decree be issued to destroy these people. Why, I am so concerned about the danger this is to you that I will even pay the cost of sending soldiers to do this to spare your royal treasury!

XERXES

(Very distracted) Yes, that sounds like a good idea. Why don't you just take care of this for me, Haman? Do what you want with those people, but keep your money. I can afford it. Here's my ring. Prepare the order!

HAMAN EXITS. CHORUS gathers around XERXES. He doesn't hear them.

CHORUS

King Xerxes, you've been taken in; you weren't very wise.

That scoundrel Haman really pulled the wool over your eyes.

You didn't stop to figure out his terrible intent,

And so the law your ring has sealed //is now set in cement.//

The laws of Medes and Persians are the laws that can't be changed,

Not even if they were thought up by someone quite deranged.

And even if the king should want to wipe it off the scroll,

Xerxes couldn't take it back, so Haman reached his goal.

Did Haman reach his goal?

XERXES EXITS.

YOUNG ESTHER

(Very upset) But, Grandma, that's awful! That nice man Mordecai is going to get killed! And what about Queen Esther? She's a Jew too. Are they going to kill her, or is she going to get away because no one knows?

GRANDMA

The story is getting exciting now, isn't it? Watch and see what happens!

ESTHER ENTERS and sits downstage left. MORDECAI ENTERS and paces in front of the palace gate, upstage. He is wearing burlap and wailing. ESTHER's MALE SERVANT ENTERS, walks past the gate, sees MORDECAI, and quickens his step. He ENTERS ESTHER's room.

SERVANT

Your majesty, Mordecai is standing at the palace gate wearing sackcloth!

ESTHER

Please get a change of clothing for him from the storeroom and take it to him. He shouldn't be dressed that way!

SERVANT

Yes, your majesty. *(He EXITS, then ENTERS a moment later, carrying a change of clothing. He approaches MORDECAI.)* Mordecai, your honor, Queen Esther is displeased to see you wearing mourning clothes, and she has sent you a set of new clothes to change into.

MORDECAI

I'm sorry, but I can't change into those clothes. A very great sorrow has come to me. Please take the clothes back to Queen Esther.

SERVANT returns to ESTHER's room.

SERVANT

Your majesty, Mordecai was not willing to take the clothes. Something is bothering him very greatly.

ESTHER

Very well. Please find Hathach and send him to me.

SERVANT

Yes, your majesty. *(EXITS)*

HATHACH ENTERS.

HATHACH

Here I am, your majesty.

ESTHER

Hathach, a great problem is disturbing Mordecai. He's at the palace gate wearing sackcloth, and has refused the new clothes I sent him. Please go and find Mordecai and ask him why he is behaving this way.

HATHACH

Yes, your majesty. *(EXITS and goes to the palace gate. To MORDECAI)* Good afternoon, Mordecai.

MORDECAI

Good afternoon, Hathach.

HATHACH

Your honor, Queen Esther is very sad to hear that you're wearing mourning clothes and don't want to change. She sent me to ask you what the problem is.

MORDECAI

Well, Hathach, Haman has cooked up a scheme to have me and all my people killed, and he has duped King Xerxes into going along with it. Haman even promised to have tons of money added to the king's treasury if we were all killed. In fact, here's a copy of the order that was read right here in Susa. Show it to Queen Esther and explain what it means. Ask her to go to the king and beg him to have pity on her people, the Jews!

HATHACH

Yes, your honor. *(Goes to ESTHER's room. To ESTHER)* Your majesty, Mordecai sent you this piece of parchment. Mordecai is sad because Haman has a plan to have all the Jewish people killed, and he talked the king into going along with his plan. The letter is sealed with the king's own ring. Mordecai would like you to go and talk to the king.

ESTHER

I see. That's very sad. But you go back and tell Mordecai this: "Everyone in Persia knows the law about people who go to see the king in his throne room. If the king has called for you, fine. But if you just decide to go on your own, the king has a law that you will be put to death—unless he decides to be nice to you. If he wants to be nice, he can pick up his gold scepter and hold it out to you. If he does that, then your life is spared. But King Xerxes seems to have forgotten about me. He hasn't asked to see me *(wailing)* for a whole month!

HATHACH

Yes, your majesty. *(Leaves and goes back to palace gate. To MORDECAI)* Well, your honor, Queen Esther says to tell you that she can't do what you ask. The law says that anyone who just shows up in the king's throne room will be put to death unless the king decides to be nice and hold out his gold scepter. She says the king hasn't asked to see her *(mimicking her)* for a whole month!

MORDECAI

Yes, I see. But you go back and tell Queen Esther: "Don't think that you're going to escape because you're the queen. If you chicken out and don't go to the king, then someone else will come along and help the Jews. But you will die, and all the rest of your family too. Who knows? Maybe you got to be queen just so you could help your people at this time."

HATHACH

Yes, your honor. *(Leaves and goes back to ESTHER's room. To ESTHER)* Your majesty, Mordecai says, "Don't think that you're going to escape because you're the queen. If you don't go to the king, then someone else will come along and help the Jews. But you will die, and all the rest of your family too. Who knows? Maybe you got to be queen just so you could help your people at this time."

ESTHER

So that's what he said, did he? I need time to think about this.

HATHACH, ESTHER, and MORDECAI FREEZE.

YOUNG ESTHER

Grandma, what did Queen Esther do? I would have been scared to death.

GRANDMA

She really had a tough choice to make, didn't she? Should she take a chance and risk her own life so she could help her people? Let's see what happened.

CHORUS

(Gathering around ESTHER) Esther faced a tough one. What course should she choose?

Go or stay, but either way she certainly could lose.

If she played the coward and stayed inside her room,

Her cousin and her family would die on the day of doom.

Esther, what's a nice Jewish girl like you doing in a Persian harem?

It was very likely that they would kill her too

If anyone let out the fact that Esther was a Jew.

But if she went to Xerxes and things went really bad,

He could order her to die, and that thought made her sad.

Esther, what IS a nice Jewish girl like you doing in a Persian harem?

ESTHER

(*Singing*) Maybe I can do it, my friends will stick with me.

They need to fast for three full days, and then we're gonna see.

But I need to use his stomach as a pathway to his heart.

I'll invite the king to dine with me, and that will be a start.

CHORUS

Esther, what's a nice Jewish girl like you doing in a Persian harem? I think maybe she just figured it out.

CHORUS crosses upstage.

ESTHER

Well, Hathach, I've made up my mind. Tell Mordecai, "Get all the Jews in Susa together and have them fast for three days for me. My servant girls and I will fast too. After the three days I'll go in to see the king, even if it means *(with a catch in her voice)* that I must die."

HATHACH

Yes, your majesty. *(Returns to the palace gate. To MORDECAI)* Well, Mordecai, Queen Esther finally said she would go to see the king. But she wants you to get all the Jews in Susa together and have them fast for three days.

MORDECAI

Ah, my Esther—she's a good girl! She has chosen well. I'll go and call my people together.

MORDECAI and HATHACH EXIT.

CHORUS

Mordecai called all the Jews.

Then he told them all the news.

He said the Queen would give a try

Even though she just might die.

So they all agreed to fast

For her until three days had passed.

SERVANT GIRL ENTERS and goes to ESTHER. They begin to primp for the big dinner.

Esther talked to her servants, and they agreed to fast.

They didn't eat a single thing until three days had passed.

They loved their pretty Esther and hoped the king would give

Her the golden scepter 'cause they wanted her to live.

XERXES ENTERS and sits on his throne, deep in thought.

ESTHER

(Whispering) Do I look all right?

SERVANT GIRL

(Whispering) Queen Esther, you look gorgeous. We've been getting ready for this moment for three days. Our thoughts are all with you.

ESTHER

Okay. Here goes nothing. If I die, I die. *(Crosses to XERXES slowly and with great dignity.)*

XERXES looks up, breaks slowly into a smile, picks up his scepter, and holds it out toward ESTHER. ESTHER continues walking up to XERXES and touches the tip of the scepter.

XERXES

Esther, what brings you here? Just ask, and I will give you anything you want, even as much as half my kingdom.

ESTHER

Your majesty, what I would like is for you and Haman to come to a dinner I will prepare for you later today.

XERXES

Servants!

HARBONA and other SERVANTS ENTER and bow.

HARBONA

Yes, your majesty?

XERXES

Hurry and get Haman so that we can accept Esther's invitation.

HARBONA

Yes, your majesty. *(Bows and EXITS.)*

ESTHER sits by XERXES. HAMAN ENTERS and sits with them. They talk silently and smile during songs.

CHORUS

Esther was most charming, as she wined and dined

The king and Haman, but she refused to speak her mind.

She asked the king and Haman to come the following day

And promised she would tell them then just what she had to say.

Haman, Haman, was so flattered to have dinner with the queen.

A man more pompous and conceited you have never ever seen.

He was also quite a racist; felt such hatred for the Jews;

Couldn't wait to terminate them on the day that he did choose.

CHORUS crosses by palace gate. MORDECAI ENTERS and stands with them. XERXES and ESTHER EXIT together. HAMAN walks slowly by gate, looking smug. All except MORDECAI bow to him, which he officiously acknowledges. HAMAN looks at MORDECAI, and his expression changes to fury, but he says nothing and stomps OFF.

ZERESH and HAMAN's 3 FRIENDS ENTER and sit downstage left. HAMAN ENTERS and joins them.

HAMAN

(Pompously) You know, I must be really important. Of course, I'm very rich, and I have 10 sons. But it's really something the way King Xerxes has honored me. Why, he made me his prime minister, and all his other officials have to treat me with the respect I so richly deserve. But that's not all. Today Queen Esther invited me to a banquet, and I was the only one besides King Xerxes who was invited. And she invit-

ed us both back tomorrow! Of course, it's only what I have coming. *(Pause)* There's only one fly in the ointment—that stinking Jew, Mordecai, who sits at the palace gate, and who never bows to me when I go in and out. Boy, I hate him, and all the other stinking Jews too.

ZERESH

But Haman, someone as important as you shouldn't let Mordecai ruin your day. You know how to get the king to do anything you want. So why don't you get rid of this guy? Do it with a flourish—with pizzazz! Give the order right away to have a tall gallows built. Then, first thing tomorrow morning, go to King Xerxes and ask him to have Mordecai hanged on it. Then you'll really be able to enjoy your dinner with the king and queen.

HAMAN'S FRIENDS

Yeah, Haman, that's the way to go.

HAMAN

Thus has it been spoken; thus shall it be done.

They all EXIT. XERXES and HARBONA ENTER from the opposite side. XERXES sits on throne. CHORUS gathers around.

XERXES

I feel crummy; I haven't slept a wink all night. (*Yawns*) So I might as well be here getting some work done. Harbona!

HARBONA

Yes, your majesty?

XERXES

Bring the records of my kingdom and read them to me!

HARBONA EXITS and returns carrying large scroll; he sits down and begins to read.

HARBONA

(*Reading*) "Bigthana and Teresh, two servants of King Xerxes, plotted to kill the king. Mordecai heard about it and told Queen Esther. His Majesty the king found that it was true, and he ordered the execution of Bigthana and Teresh. They were hanged on the tenth day of the eighth month."

XERXES

(*Interrupting*) Tell me, what has been done to reward Mordecai for saving my life?

HARBONA

Nothing, your majesty.

HAMAN ENTERS to one side, standing just at the edge of the stage.

XERXES

(*Glancing to the side*) Who is that man waiting out there?

HARBONA

Your majesty, it's Haman.

XERXES

Have him come in!

HARBONA goes to the side and speaks to HAMAN. HAMAN crosses to XERXES.

XERXES

Haman, what should I do for a man I want to honor?

HAMAN

Well, your majesty, let me think about this a bit.

CHORUS

Haman, Haman, you're so evil, you were waiting to demand

That King Xerxes should deliver Mordecai into your hand.

You'd be very glad to hang him from the gallows way up high,

And then finally be rid of disrespectful Mordecai.

But you also are conceited, really such a pompous fool.

"The one King Xerxes wants to honor must be me," you thought, "How cool!

What would make me feel important? Something splashy, yes, of course.

I'll be taken through the city riding Xerxes' finest horse."

HAMAN

Your majesty, here's what I think you should do for the man you want to honor. Dress the man in your own royal robe, and let him ride your own royal horse with all its royal trappings. Then have one of your most trusted officials lead the horse through the streets proclaiming, "This is what King Xerxes does for the man he wants to honor!"

XERXES

Thus has it been spoken; thus shall it be done. Hurry! Go and get the robe and the horse and do everything you just said for a man who sits at the gate—Mordecai!

HAMAN is aghast. He EXITS slowly and sadly.

CHORUS

Haman, Haman, so self-serving, you gave the king your own advice,

Then your clever scheme turned sour—Mordecai got treated nice.

You had to put the king's own clothing on your enemy the Jew;

Mount him on King Xerxes' horse, and lead him all the city through.

Haman, Haman, how you hated to act nice to Mordecai.

It made you so grossed out and angry that you thought you'd rather die.

How you wanted to be noticed, to be honored and revered,

Wearing all those fancy clothes and smiling as the people cheered.

All EXIT except CHORUS.

CHORUS

Mordecai was unimpressed

At just how fancy he was dressed.

Fancy dress was not his style,

But he smiled a secret smile

About this honor when he saw

How it stuck in Haman's craw.

ZERESH and HAMAN's FRIENDS ENTER, talking and laughing. They sit. HAMAN ENTERS and joins them.

HAMAN

You guys just won't believe the awful experience I had this morning. I was on my way to see the king to ask him to have Mordecai hanged. But before I could open my mouth, he asked me what he should do for a person he really wants to honor. Well, I thought he wanted to give me more of the honor I so richly deserve, so I told him what I would enjoy. I told him to dress that person in the king's robe and put him on the king's horse and lead him through the city, saying, "This is what the king does for the man he wants to honor!" I was so pleased that I had come up with such a great idea, and I was really looking forward to riding that horse. And then, to my absolute horror, the king told me to do that for, of all people, that Jew Mordecai. I didn't have a choice. And the worst of it is that I think Mordecai thought it was kind of funny—my hating it, I mean.

ZERESH

Oh, Haman, I get cold shivers when you say that. I am really scared for you. If Mordecai is a Jew, you had better watch out!

HARBONA ENTERS with other SERVANTS.

HARBONA

It's time for Queen Esther's banquet. King Xerxes sent us to get Haman right away.

All but CHORUS EXIT.

ESTHER, XERXES, and HAMAN ENTER and sit as if at a party.

ESTHER

I hope your excellency is enjoying your dinner. Would you like to have more wine? And how about you, Haman?

XERXES

I know there is something on your mind, Queen Esther. What can I get for you? Just ask, and I'll give you whatever you want, up to half of my kingdom.

ESTHER

Your majesty, if you really love me and want to help me, then please save me and my people! That's what I really want. You see, a reward has been promised to anyone who kills my people. If we were only going to be sold as slaves, I wouldn't have bothered you.

XERXES

Who in the world would dare to do such a thing?

ESTHER

The one out to get us is—none other than wicked Haman!

HAMAN looks terrified, glancing from ESTHER to XERXES and back again. XERXES looks furious, gets up, and stomps off to one side. HAMAN looks desperate, then gets an idea. He kneels beside ESTHER to beg for his life. XERXES returns and looks at HAMAN.

XERXES

Now you're trying to win my queen, right here in my own palace. Just who do you think you are?

HARBONA and other SERVANTS ENTER.

HARBONA

Your majesty, Haman has built a very tall gallows next to his house so he could hang Mordecai on it. Mordecai, the very one who spoke up and saved your life.

XERXES

Hang Haman from his own gallows! *(Snaps his fingers)*

HARBONA

Thus have you spoken, your majesty; thus shall it be done.

All EXIT during song except XERXES, ESTHER, and CHORUS.

CHORUS

Haman, Haman, oh so pompous, claiming to be such a friend

To King Xerxes, you've been caught now, and you've come to such an end.

Haman, Haman, you are swinging from the gallows you had made,

And you really had it coming for the nasty trap you laid.

(More slowly) Haman, Haman, oh so pompous, claiming to be such a friend

To King Xerxes, you've been caught now, and you've come to such an end.

XERXES

Well, Esther, we got rid of that scoundrel Haman. I want you to take all Haman's riches now.

ESTHER

Your majesty, there is something that you should know. Mordecai is my cousin. He is the one who brought me up when my parents died.

XERXES

Were you afraid to tell me that? But it's all right. I owe my life to your cousin. I'm going to promote him to take Haman's place as prime minister.

ESTHER

Thank you, your majesty. *(EXITS)*

MORDECAI ENTERS.

MORDECAI

You summoned me, your majesty?

XERXES

Yes, Mordecai. I hereby appoint you to Haman's job as my prime minister. Here's my ring for you to wear.

Gives MORDECAI his ring. MORDECAI takes it and EXITS. XERXES sits on throne.

CHORUS

Haman, Haman, you are dead now, but the evil law you made
Can't be canceled ever, ever, and the Jews are still afraid.
So Queen Esther isn't finished; she still has some work to do,
One more visit to the throne room, just to see this business through.

ESTHER ENTERS in tears and falls at XERXES' feet.

ESTHER

(Wailing) Please stop Haman's evil plan to have all us Jews killed!

XERXES holds out golden scepter and ESTHER stands up.

ESTHER

Your majesty, I know that you will do the right thing, and that you really love me. Please stop what Haman has planned! He has already sent letters demanding the Jews be killed in all the places you rule over. I can't bear to see all my people destroyed!

MORDECAI ENTERS.

XERXES

I've already killed Haman, but I can see that didn't solve the problem. The law he made is still in effect, and even I can't undo it. But here's what we can do. We can make another law that lets your people fight back, and you can seal it with my ring.

CROWD ENTERS and mills around with XERXES, ESTHER, and MORDECAI. TOWN CRIER ENTERS and opens scroll.

TOWN CRIER

(Reading) Hear ye, hear ye, it is proclaimed that on the thirteenth day of Adar, the Jews can gather and defend themselves against anyone who attacks them. They may kill their enemies and take their possessions.

LISTENER 1

Did you hear that?

LISTENER 2

(Whistles)

LISTENER 3

All right! We're saved!

LISTENER 1

Let's go tell everyone the good news!

LISTENER 2

Let's plan a big party!

LISTENER 3

Yeah. Let's go!

CHORUS

Haman, Haman, all your scheming didn't work out as you planned.
The Jews attacked their persecutors all throughout the Persian land.
And the Jews were all so happy that you didn't get your way.
So each year they celebrate this on their Purim holiday.

King Xerxes was a party king, but his kingdom ran just fine;
The work was done by Mordecai //while Xerxes drank his wine.//

Mordecai was famous too.
He made it cool to be a Jew.

He earned the Persians' high regard
By being fair and working hard.
Had favor in all Jewish eyes
Because he was so good and wise.

Esther, the nice Jewish girl, became the Persian queen,
And when she got the job, she didn't know what it would mean.
She faced a mighty challenge; took it strong and bold,
And ever since throughout the world her story now is told.
Esther, what WAS a nice Jewish girl like you doing in a Persian harem?
Esther, you were present at just the time and place
Where you were needed crucially to rescue all your race.
Mordecai suggested just what it all could mean,
And have you figured out by now just who had you made queen?

GRANDMA

And so that's what Queen Esther did back in Persia 2,000 years ago. What do you think of her?

YOUNG ESTHER

She was pretty gutsy! I'm glad my name is Esther too.

CHORUS

He's got the whole world in His hands.
He's got the whole wide world in His hands.
He's got the whole world in His hands.
He's got the whole world in His hands.
///He's got pretty Queen Esther in His hands.///
He's got the whole world in His hands.
///He's got the Jewish people in His hands.///
He's got the whole world in His hands.
///He's got you and me in His hands.///
He's got the whole world in His hands.

Cast and audience join in on repeat of first verse. Cast EXITS.

What's a Nice Jewish Girl Like You Doing in a Persian Harem?

by Barbara Hollenbach

A Note to the Pastor or Teacher:

Esther can be held up as an example of courage in the face of hardship but Esther, like other biblical greats, is shown to have sinful human actions. Besides hiding who she was—a chosen member of a chosen race, redeemed by God from Egypt and Babylon—she seems to have violated Mosaic Law on matters of purity and marriage. God's care for His children and His control of historical events should not be used to cover up this fact.

In truth, the real hero in Esther's story is God. It does seem that Esther was the right person at the right time, but we should remember that God made Esther a special person; Esther was one part in God's plan of salvation. Likewise, each of God's baptized children are heroes. We are part of God's plan of salvation won for us in Christ Jesus. Each of us is working in the kingdom to tell our friends, coworkers, government officials, and all others the story of Jesus' death and resurrection.

Questions for Study and Discussion:

1. What does the story of Esther teach us about God our Father?

2. Describe how each of the main characters used their positions or talents to achieve their desires.

3. In what way could Esther's story happen today?

InterMission Scripts

InterMission Scripts are a dynamic way to get people to sit up and take notice in your services. They're short (five to ten minutes long) and use natural dialogue, easy staging and a limited number of performers. The information you need—time, cast, costumes, props, sound, lighting and setting—is on the first page for quick reference. Each Christ-centered script includes a clearly stated purpose, theme, Scripture reference and discussion questions.

REPRODUCiBLE unlimited, **ROYALTY-FREE** use!

Wearing the Mask: Dramas for Youth
Deals with real-life issues: peer pressure, dating, being responsible, witnessing, more. *13 scripts*
ISBN 0-570-05376-5   12-3427 $14.99

Strong and Sturdy: Dramas for Children
One full-length play based on the book of Esther, plus three others, 3–7 minutes long. *4 scripts*
ISBN 0-570-05389-7   12-4016 $12.99

Fearless Pharoah FooFoo and Other Dramas for Children
Dramas for 6- to 12-year-olds. Minimal preparation; maximum enjoyment. *34 scripts*
ISBN 0-570-05332-3   12-3380 $14.99

Command Performances: Playing with the Ten Commandments
11 simple scripts make learning the Ten Commandments child's play for children ages 6–12.
ISBN 0-570-05370-6   12-3421 $12.99

Anticipation: Dramas for Advent
Discover the significance of time spent awaiting the birth of Christ through these living reflections on the meaning of God's arrival among His people. *14 scripts*
ISBN 0-570-05386-2   12-4014 $12.99

Celebration: Dramas for Christmas
Reflect on the meaning of Christ's birth to you personally—and the role you play each day as a follower of Christ—with these thoughtful, funny, joy-filled Christmas dramas. *7 scripts*
ISBN 0-570-05387-0   12-4015 $12.99

Preparation: Dramas for Lent
Gain a more personal understanding of the utter helplessness and fear early Christians experienced as they watched Christ crucified—until the moment they knew He had risen for them. *8 scripts*
ISBN 0-570-05391-9   12-4018 $12.99

Jubilation: Dramas for Easter
Cut through the clutter and distractions of daily life. Use these dramas to turn a spotlight on the single event that makes every moment of every day a cause for hope and joy. *7 scripts*
ISBN 0-570-05390-0   12-4017 $12.99

(Excerpt from Fearless Pharaoh Foo Foo)

Fearless Pharaoh FooFoo

Text: Exodus 5:1–14:31

Level: Grades 1–4

Participants: Narrator, Pharaoh, Pharaoh's Son, Moses, Frogs, Gnats, Bugs, Cows, Locusts, Israelites.

Props: Glass or pitcher and red food coloring; two pieces of poster board; blue cloth or sheet; a whip.

Notes: Use as many children as possible as frogs, gnats, bugs, cows, locusts, and Israelites. Have some children throw Wiffle balls or ping pong balls as hail. The sea is a blue cloth held by two children. The refrain is sung/chanted to the tune used in the children's rhyme "Little Bunny Foo Foo." The words can be printed on poster board and held up for the audience to join in.

Setting the Stage: *PHARAOH is seated on a throne centerstage. He holds a whip. One or two ISRAELITE SLAVES are working fearfully in front of PHARAOH. PHARAOH has his SON by his side. The SON sneers and makes faces throughout the scene. PHARAOH has a clear pitcher or glass of water on a table by his hand. MOSES turns the water red (using food coloring) for the first plague. Other plagues are acted out by individual children hopping like frogs, biting and buzzing, etc. Two or more children stand off to the side, holding a blue cloth or sheet to represent the sea.*

PHARAOH

I'm the Pharaoh of all Egypt—that's king to you, stupids! And I ain't afraid of anybody!

NARRATOR

Sounds brave and bold, but it might not be too smart! Even though he's king of all Egypt, there's probably Somebody he should respect and even fear enough to obey.

ALL

(Chanted) Fearless Pharaoh FooFoo, rulin' rich old Egypt,
Picking on the Israelites and working them to death.

NARRATOR

When along came the prophet Moses, and he said,

ALL

Fearless Pharaoh FooFoo, I don't like your attitude
Picking on the Israelites and working them to death.

NARRATOR

Let my people go! God is giving you 10 chances, and if you can't learn to behave, He'll drown you in the sea!

ALL

Fearless Pharaoh FooFoo, rulin' rich old Egypt,
Picking on the Israelites and working them to death.

PHARAOH reaches for the glass or pitcher of water, slips food coloring in it—without the audience seeing—so it turns red. He picks up the glass to drink from it, sees that it's turned red, makes a face, and puts the glass back down. This happens as NARRATOR says the next line.

NARRATOR

When along came the prophet Moses—turning the river water red—and he said,

ALL

Fearless Pharaoh FooFoo, I don't like your attitude,
Picking on the Israelites and working them to death.

NARRATOR

God is giving you nine more chances, and if you can't learn to behave, He'll drown you in the sea!

ALL

Fearless Pharaoh FooFoo, rulin' rich old Egypt,
Picking on the Israelites and working them to death.

NARRATOR

When along came the prophet Moses—with flippy, floppy frogs—and he said,

ALL

Fearless Pharaoh FooFoo, I don't like your attitude,
Picking on the Israelites and working them to death.

NARRATOR

God is giving you eight more chances, and if you can't learn to behave, He'll drown you in the sea!

ALL

Fearless Pharaoh FooFoo, rulin' rich old Egypt,
Picking on the Israelites and working them to death.

(Excerpt from Command Performances)

7
Dumb-De-Dumb-Dumb, David

"You shall not commit adultery."
The Sixth Commandment (L/RC)
The Seventh Commandment (Prot/Orth)

Text: 2 Samuel 11–12

Level: Kindergarten and up

Participants: Narrator[s], Chorus, David, Conscience, Servant, Bathsheba, Uriah, Nathan

Props: Bench or cot for rooftop scene, chair for throne, play money, paper for messages; costumes and poster board are optional.

Sound: Stationary mikes for Reader, Conscience, and Narrator[s]; lapel mikes for David and Nathan

Notes: Reader and Narrator are at microphones. When very young kids do this, the chorus or a speaker offstage can recite the commandments that are repeated here, rather than having those lines spoken by Conscience. The songs are optional. The Chorus' line, "Dumb-de-dumb-dumb, David!" can be sung to the "suspense tone" (d, e, f, d, g$^\#$, a) used often in old movies and TV shows to indicate trouble.

The NARRATOR stands to one side. DAVID is centerstage on the cot with the SERVANT near. CONSCIENCE is also lounging near DAVID. The NARRATOR is very romantic at the beginning, but gradually comes to see the tawdriness of David's actions. CONSCIENCE quite consistently interrupts the NARRATOR. DAVID shows no recognition of CONSCIENCE's presence until he pushes CONSCIENCE aside.

NARRATOR
(To audience) You may remember this story. *(Dramatically)* It's a story of passion and romance and the struggle of forbidden love!

CONSCIENCE
(To audience, with a scathing look at NARRATOR) Hardly! I should know! I am David's conscience and trust me—it was less about passion and romance than plain old dumb lust and disobedience of the sixth [seventh] Commandment. Just watch.

NARRATOR

(Picking up the Bible) Listen to how it begins. It's so romantic. "One evening David got up from his bed and walked around on the roof of the palace. From the roof he saw a woman bathing. The woman was very beautiful" *(2 Samuel 11:2–3).*

DAVID sits up, walks about, looks out, and calls the SERVANT to his side, pointing into the distance.

DAVID
(Sung to "Deck the Halls") Who's that bathing beauty yonder?

CHORUS
(Sung) Oo-la-la-la-la, la-la-la-la!

DAVID
(Sung) She's so lovely—makes me wonder:

CHORUS
(Sung) Oo-la-la-la-la, la-la-la-la!

DAVID
(Sung) I'm the king, won't that impress her?

CHORUS
(Sung) Oo-la-la, Oo-la-la, la la la!

DAVID
(Sung) Rank and wealth, they add their pressure.

CHORUS
(Sung) Oo-la-la-la-la, la-la-la-la!

The SERVANT whispers to DAVID.

NARRATOR
(Spoken) David's servants told him that the bathing beauty was—

CONSCIENCE
Bathsheba, and she's married—you are too!

DAVID
(Glibly) But I'm the king!

CHORUS
(Spoken or chanted rhythmically, a la the "Dragnet" theme song) Dumb-De-Dumb-Dumb, David!

NARRATOR
David knew the commandments of God. He knew that:

DAVID paces thoughtfully, making a decision.